By Laura Williams
Translated by Lee Ji-su

© 2022 Williams Books
1 rue de l'église, 91430 Igny
Dépôt légal : Décembre 2022
ISBN 978-2-494614-43-7
Imprimé à la demande par Amazon
Loi n° 49-956 du 16 juillet 1949 sur les publications destinées à la jeunesse

사과

[sagwa] – apple

아보카도

[abokado] – avocado

바나나

[banana] - banana

콩

[kong] - beans

양배추

[yangbaechu] - cabbage

당근

[dang-geun] - carrot

고추

[gochu] – chilli

옥수수

[ogsusu] - corn

오이

[oi] - cucumber

가지

[gaji] – eggplant

마늘

[maneul] – garlic

생강

[saeng-gang] - ginger

강낭콩

[gangnangkong] - green beans

구아바

[guaba] – guava

레몬

[lemon] - lemon

망고

[mang-go] - mango

버섯

[beoseos] - mushroom

양파

[yangpa] – onion

오렌지

[olenji] – orange

파파야

[papaya] - papaya

패션프루트

[paesyeonpeuluteu] – passion fruit

땅콩

[ttangkong] - peanut

완두콩

[wandukong] - peas

파인애플

[pain-aepeul] - pineapple

감자

[gamja] - potato

호박

[hobag] - pumpkin

쌀

[ssal] - rice

간장

[ganjang] – soy

시금치

[sigeumchi] – spinach

사탕 수수

[satang susu] – sugar cane

고구마

[goguma] - sweet potato

토마토

[tomato] - tomato

수박

[subag] - watermelon

밀

[mil] - wheat

Thank you

Thank you for purchasing "Korean-English Words for Toddlers"! Your support means a lot to me, and I hope you and your child enjoy these books.

If you have a moment, I would greatly appreciate it if you could leave a review on Amazon. Your feedback will help me improve future editions of the series and create more resources for bilingual children.

Thank you again for your support. You can access the reviews on Amazon by scanning the QR code below or by visiting the link below:

https://www.amazon.com/review/create-review?&asin=2494614430

Thank you for helping me continue my work as a language teacher and translator. Your support is greatly appreciated!

In the same collection

www.ingramcontent.com/pod-product-compliance
Lightning Source LLC
LaVergne TN
LVHW071654180726
843512LV00002B/450